What Went Well?
Journal

Daily reminders of the good in your life, and the good that you bring to the world.

Write about it. *Think* about it. *Be* about it.

Date Gifted: _____

Name: _____

Address: _____

City: _____ State: _____ Zip: _____

Home Phone: _____

Cell Phone: _____

Work Phone: _____

Clean Sweep Publishing

Copyright © 2020 Lisa Summerour, Ed.D.

Published by Clean Sweep Publishing, LLC

Edited by April Casey, MAE

Graphic Design by Dave Kinzel

Phone: 442.444.0070 | Fax: 708.545.1157
www.cleansweeppublishing.com

All rights reserved. No part of this book may be reproduced in any form or by any means, including photocopying, without written permission from the publisher.

Printed in the United States of America.

What Went Well?

*To my mother, Jacqueline Elaine Magruder Perry
for always reminding us to **"Think good thoughts…"***

*To my dad, Charles Fulton Perry Sr. who encouraged me to
write, and who often entered a room with,
"Tell me something good!"*

*To my biological father,
William Sherman Summerour Jr. for one of his favorite
phrases, **"Do Something About it!"***

*To my heart's joy, Gregory Manning Wachter, for your light,
love, laughter, and lullabies …**"Are you kidding me?!"***

Table of Contents

How To Use Your *What Went Well?* Journal	1
Activity #1: Character Strengths Assessment	13
Activity #2: Meditation	25
Activity #3: Financial Freedom Requires Your Full Engagement	37
Activity #4: Review Your Character Strengths	49
Activity #5: Eating Well or Eating Better – Pick One!	61
Activity #6: Physical Well-being	73
Activity #7: Mental Wellness	85
Activity #8: Write Your Mission Statement	97
Activity #9: Give Thanks and Thank Yous	109
Activity #10: Purpose, Pleasure & Perspective	121
Activity #11: Be a Tourist in Your Town!	133
Activity #12: 12 Months of What Went Well!	145

Welcome

Welcome to your *What Went Well?* Journal. This journal is designed to help you think about the things that go well in your life every day. This daily exercise is based on research done by positive psychologist, Dr. Martin E. P. Seligman, as presented in his book, *Flourish: A Visionary New Understanding of Happiness and Wellbeing*. Many estimate that approximately 70% of our daily thoughts are negative. Consider the thoughts and emotions you devote to what has gone right in your life, as compared to what's gone wrong. When was the last time you called a friend and spent 20-minutes railing about how right everything went that day? Exactly!

I created the *What Went Well?* Journal because I was absolutely intrigued with the idea of being intentional about focusing on the good things that happen to us, around us, and because of us - daily. This journal is designed to help you recall, reflect, and reconnect with things that are going well, all the good stuff you experience that might otherwise slip by unnoticed. This book doesn't erase bad and unpleasant experiences, they are a part of life. This *What Went Well?* Journal can help you avoid allowing bad and unpleasant experiences to take over your day, your week, or your life.

> ### Important Wellness Message
>
> *I am not a mental health professional, and this journal is not a substitute for treatment of any ailments or mental health issues. I am someone who wants to see every person empowered to live more joyfully, by examining the good in his or her world - on purpose!*
>
> *If you or someone you know is struggling with depression or any other mental health challenge, please seek professional medical attention. If you are under the care of a mental health professional, I encourage you to notify them that you are using this journal. Let them know that its purpose is to create awareness of the positive experiences happening in your life.*
>
> *If you or someone you know appears to be a health risk, by putting themselves or others in danger, please call 911 for immediate care, support, or intervention.*

How to use your *What Went Well?* Journal

Using your journal is simple!

On the **left page** you will identify 3 good things that happened during the day and write them down.

EXAMPLE:

Sunday

Renee had a great interview today!

Tami was approved to rent the office for her new business.

April's sons and husband treated her to a movie and dinner.

On the **right page**, write why or how the three things on the left page happened. What was it that caused them to work out well?

EXAMPLE:

Renee practiced for her interview ahead of time and was well-prepared.

Tami wrote a very good letter of interest showing herself a good tenant.

April is a great mom & wife, and her family really appreciates her.

Sunday

The *What Went Well?* Journal is designed for you to begin using on any day of the week, and any time of the year. Put the date in the upper left corner, or put it anywhere you'd like, and get started.

This is a new activity, so for now, leave this book on your pillow or some place you are sure to see it each night so you remember to write. Once you get your first week under your belt, you'll be on your way to months of *What Went Well?* experiences.

What Went Well?

Date: _____ **Write down 3 things** that went well.

Sunday

Monday

Tuesday

Wednesday

Thursday

Friday

Saturday

Why did these things go well?

Sunday

Monday

Tuesday

Wednesday

Thursday

Friday

Saturday

What Went Well?

Date: _____ **Write down 3 things** that went well.

- Sunday
- Monday
- Tuesday
- Wednesday
- Thursday
- Friday
- Saturday

Why did these things go well?

Sunday

Monday

Tuesday

Wednesday

Thursday

Friday

Saturday

What Went Well?

Date: _____ **Write down 3 things** that went well.

Sunday

Monday

Tuesday

Wednesday

Thursday

Friday

Saturday

Why did these things go well?

Sunday

Monday

Tuesday

Wednesday

Thursday

Friday

Saturday

What Went Well?

Date: _____ **Write down 3 things** that went well.

Sunday

Monday

Tuesday

Wednesday

Thursday

Friday

Saturday

Why did these things go well?

Sunday

Monday

Tuesday

Wednesday

Thursday

Friday

Saturday

What Went Well?

Date: _____ **Write down 3 things that went well.**

Sunday

Monday

Tuesday

Wednesday

Thursday

Friday

Saturday

Why did these things go well?

Sunday

Monday

Tuesday

Wednesday

Thursday

Friday

Saturday

What Went Well?

Imagine yourself strong
**LIVING VIBRANTLY
LOVING YOU AND
BEING LOVED
EXCITED ABOUT TODAY.**

— *Go!* —

•••

Dr. Lisa Summerour

ACTIVITY #1
Character Strengths Assessment

I have taken quite a few assessments over the years, and the Strengths Assessment is by far one of my favorites because it assesses your character strengths, which are also known as your best qualities.

The Character Strengths Assessment is owned by the VIA Institute, and a FREE version is available on their website, which is provided below! Other versions are available for purchase. The website shares this:

> When you discover your greatest strengths, you learn to use them to handle stress and life challenges, become happier, and develop relationships with those who matter most to you. What are your strengths?

There is an assessment designed for adults and another for children between the ages of 10 and 17. After you complete your assessment, write your top seven (7) character strengths here:

1. _____
2. _____
3. _____
4. _____
5. _____
6. _____
7. _____

Visit: *www.viacharacter.org* to access and complete the Character Strengths Survey.

Date: _____ **Write down 3 things** that went well.

Sunday

Monday

Tuesday

Wednesday

Thursday

Friday

Saturday

Why did these things go well?

Sunday

Monday

Tuesday

Wednesday

Thursday

Friday

Saturday

Date: _____ **Write down 3 things** that went well.

Sunday

Monday

Tuesday

Wednesday

Thursday

Friday

Saturday

Why did these things go well?

- Sunday
- Monday
- Tuesday
- Wednesday
- Thursday
- Friday
- Saturday

What Went Well?

Date: _____ **Write down 3 things that went well.**

Sunday

Monday

Tuesday

Wednesday

Thursday

Friday

Saturday

Why did these things go well?

Sunday

Monday

Tuesday

Wednesday

Thursday

Friday

Saturday

What Went Well?

Date: _____ **Write down 3 things** that went well.

Sunday

Monday

Tuesday

Wednesday

Thursday

Friday

Saturday

Why did these things go well?

Sunday

Monday

Tuesday

Wednesday

Thursday

Friday

Saturday

What Went Well?

Date: _____ **Write down 3 things** that went well.

Sunday	
Monday	
Tuesday	
Wednesday	
Thursday	
Friday	
Saturday	

Why did these things go well?

- Sunday
- Monday
- Tuesday
- Wednesday
- Thursday
- Friday
- Saturday

What Went Well?

SO FAR YOU'VE *conquered every* CHALLENGE LIFE HAS PRESENTED. NICELY DONE. YOU ARE *amazing!*

• • •

Dr. Lisa Summerour

ACTIVITY #2
Meditation

Meditation is a technique used to rest or clear the mind. Meditating is not a religion, although some religions do incorporate meditation into their faith. Otherwise, meditation can be practiced in addition to prayer.

There are many benefits to meditating, including:

- Reducing cortisol levels
- Lowering stress
- Promoting a more positive outlook
- Lower blood pressure
- Improve immune system
- Increase compassion toward others
- Increase memory, speech, and ability to focus
- Help regulate emotions

I encourage you to research the different types of meditation and experiment until you find one that works for you. For now, here is a quick and easy meditation exercise you can do.

Take 5 or 10 minutes and focus on your breathing. Sit comfortably, close your eyes, and inhale for 2 seconds, hold your breath for 2 seconds, then exhale for 4 seconds. Or, inhale for 3, hold for 3, and exhale for 6. Practice this for 5 to 10 minutes a day for one week.

Date: _____ **Write down 3 things** that went well.

Sunday

Monday

Tuesday

Wednesday

Thursday

Friday

Saturday

Why did these things go well?

Sunday

Monday

Tuesday

Wednesday

Thursday

Friday

Saturday

What Went Well?

Date: _____ **Write down 3 things** that went well.

Sunday

Monday

Tuesday

Wednesday

Thursday

Friday

Saturday

Why did these things go well?

Sunday

Monday

Tuesday

Wednesday

Thursday

Friday

Saturday

Date: _____ **Write down 3 things that went well.**

Sunday

Monday

Tuesday

Wednesday

Thursday

Friday

Saturday

Why did these things go well?

Sunday

Monday

Tuesday

Wednesday

Thursday

Friday

Saturday

What Went Well?

Date: _____ **Write down 3 things** that went well.

Sunday

Monday

Tuesday

Wednesday

Thursday

Friday

Saturday

Why did these things go well?

Sunday

Monday

Tuesday

Wednesday

Thursday

Friday

Saturday

What Went Well?

Date: _____ **Write down 3 things** that went well.

- Sunday
- Monday
- Tuesday
- Wednesday
- Thursday
- Friday
- Saturday

Why did these things go well?

Sunday

Monday

Tuesday

Wednesday

Thursday

Friday

Saturday

What Went Well?

BRING WHAT YOU HAVE TO DO WHAT YOU CAN AND YOUR SINCERE *effort will be* APPRECIATED.

...

Dr. Lisa Summerour

ACTIVITY #3
Financial Freedom Requires Your Full Engagement

My grandmother used to say there is a difference between being broke and being in debt. The truth is neither is good if both are constant aspects of your day-to-day, or week-to-week reality. If you are always broke and living pay-check-to-pay-check, there's a problem. If you are in debt and have no plan to get out from under it, that too is a problem.

It is your responsibility to get actively engaged in taking control of your financial situation. If you've already thought or said out loud, "I just need more money!" then, you need to reset your thinking. Maybe you will get more money, but you will be better prepared to handle more money when you learn to respect and appreciate the money you make now.

I am recommending the book, *Say Yes to No Debt: 12 Steps to Financial Freedom* by Reverend Dr. DeForest B. Soaries. I am recommending this book because the financial education program Dr. Soaries implemented at his church has helped hundreds of people go debt free. People have found freedom because they replaced a "get more" mindset with a "get out of debt" lifestyle.

Get a copy of the book for approximately $10; less if you purchase an ebook. You can also visit *mydfree.org* for information and resources to help you get fully engaged in designing a financial future that makes you proud.

Date: _____ **Write down 3 things** that went well.

Sunday

Monday

Tuesday

Wednesday

Thursday

Friday

Saturday

Why did these things go well?

Sunday

Monday

Tuesday

Wednesday

Thursday

Friday

Saturday

Date: _____ **Write down 3 things** that went well.

- Sunday
- Monday
- Tuesday
- Wednesday
- Thursday
- Friday
- Saturday

Why did these things go well?

Sunday

Monday

Tuesday

Wednesday

Thursday

Friday

Saturday

What Went Well?

Date: _____ **Write down 3 things** that went well.

Sunday

Monday

Tuesday

Wednesday

Thursday

Friday

Saturday

Why did these things go well?

Sunday

Monday

Tuesday

Wednesday

Thursday

Friday

Saturday

What Went Well?

Date: _____ **Write down 3 things** that went well.

Sunday

Monday

Tuesday

Wednesday

Thursday

Friday

Saturday

Why did these things go well?

Sunday

Monday

Tuesday

Wednesday

Thursday

Friday

Saturday

What Went Well?

Date: _____ **Write down 3 things** that went well.

- Sunday
- Monday
- Tuesday
- Wednesday
- Thursday
- Friday
- Saturday

Why did these things go well?

Sunday

Monday

Tuesday

Wednesday

Thursday

Friday

Saturday

DOING WHAT YOU LOVE IS **THE HARD WORK THAT** *energizes you.* **GET UP AND GET TO IT!**

...

Dr. Lisa Summerour

ACTIVITY #4
Review Your Character Strengths

In Activity #1 you had the opportunity to take the VIA Institute's Character Strengths Assessment.

Write the top three (3) character strengths from Activity #1 here:

1. _____
2. _____
3. _____

Take some time to reflect on the past few months and answer the following questions:

What resonated with you about one or all of your top three character strengths?

Give an example of how positively one of these strengths has served you or shown up in your life.

Write down what you love about this strength in your life.

Date: _____ **Write down 3 things** that went well.

- Sunday
- Monday
- Tuesday
- Wednesday
- Thursday
- Friday
- Saturday

Why did these things go well?

Sunday

Monday

Tuesday

Wednesday

Thursday

Friday

Saturday

Date: _____ **Write down 3 things that went well.**

Sunday

Monday

Tuesday

Wednesday

Thursday

Friday

Saturday

Why did these things go well?

Sunday

Monday

Tuesday

Wednesday

Thursday

Friday

Saturday

What Went Well?

Date: _____ **Write down 3 things** that went well.

- Sunday
- Monday
- Tuesday
- Wednesday
- Thursday
- Friday
- Saturday

Why did these things go well?

Sunday

Monday

Tuesday

Wednesday

Thursday

Friday

Saturday

What Went Well?

Date: _____ **Write down 3 things** that went well.

Sunday

Monday

Tuesday

Wednesday

Thursday

Friday

Saturday

Why did these things go well?

Sunday

Monday

Tuesday

Wednesday

Thursday

Friday

Saturday

Date: _____ **Write down 3 things** that went well.

Sunday

Monday

Tuesday

Wednesday

Thursday

Friday

Saturday

Why did these things go well?

- Sunday
- Monday
- Tuesday
- Wednesday
- Thursday
- Friday
- Saturday

What Went Well?

A breakthrough is **WHEN YOU REALIZE** YOU CAN LIVE WITHOUT IT.

AN ABUNDANT BREAKTHROUGH *is when you embrace that* **YOU WILL LIVE** *better without it.*

Dr. Lisa Summerour

ACTIVITY #5
Eating Well or Eating Better – Pick One!

Whether it's feeling good, looking great, or thinking with increased clarity what we put in our bodies matters.

Your activity for this period is all about eating better. Now is an excellent time to schedule a physical exam. Ask your doctor to include a nutritional assessment if at all possible.

If you've been experiencing anything that might require a mental health practitioner, now is the time to address that as well. Again, based on your insurance, etc. ask your primary care physician for a referral and check with your insurance provider.

Here are a few things you can do immediately to start down the road to better eating:

- Clean out your refrigerator and your food cabinets. Remove junk food, old/expired foods, and anything you already know you aren't supposed to be eating.

- Stop purchasing foods you should not eat.

- Add three things to your diet that are healthier choices and include a healthy snack.

- Drink enough water. What does that even mean anymore? Amy Marturana's article should help.[1]

Don't beat yourself up. Start where you are, and make improvements. You got this! Celebrate your decision to engage in better eating.

---

[1] Amy Marturana, *Here's Exactly How Much Water You Should Drink Every Day*, Self.com, January 2, 2019, accessed June 23, 2019.

Date: _____ **Write down 3 things** that went well.

Sunday

Monday

Tuesday

Wednesday

Thursday

Friday

Saturday

Why did these things go well?

Sunday

Monday

Tuesday

Wednesday

Thursday

Friday

Saturday

What Went Well?

Date: _____ **Write down 3 things that went well.**

Sunday

Monday

Tuesday

Wednesday

Thursday

Friday

Saturday

Why did these things go well?

Sunday

Monday

Tuesday

Wednesday

Thursday

Friday

Saturday

What Went Well?

Date: _____   **Write down 3 things** that went well.

Sunday

Monday

Tuesday

Wednesday

Thursday

Friday

Saturday

Why did these things go well?

Sunday

Monday

Tuesday

Wednesday

Thursday

Friday

Saturday

Date: _____ **Write down 3 things** that went well.

Sunday

Monday

Tuesday

Wednesday

Thursday

Friday

Saturday

Why did these things go well?

Sunday

Monday

Tuesday

Wednesday

Thursday

Friday

Saturday

What Went Well?

Date: _____ **Write down 3 things** that went well.

Sunday	
Monday	
Tuesday	
Wednesday	
Thursday	
Friday	
Saturday	

Why did these things go well?

Sunday

Monday

Tuesday

Wednesday

Thursday

Friday

Saturday

What Went Well?

You can change today.
IN THIS MOMENT YOU CAN PURPOSE THAT THE **NEXT MOMENT WILL BE DECIDEDLY DIFFERENT. THE CHOICE IS,** AND ALWAYS HAS BEEN, *yours to make.* THE TIME TO MAKE IT IS *always now.*

...

Dr. Lisa Summerour

ACTIVITY #6
Physical Well-being

Physical well-being is about getting active and listening to your body. The options are endless:

- Join a gym.
- Get a trainer - for home or at your gym.
- Walk/Jog/Run – depending on your ability – start by walking around your block, your house, or from the porch to the sidewalk. Just get started!
- Get a work-out partner – The buddy system is powerful!
- Dance – You can do it at home anytime you want.
- Swim, or consider water aerobics.
- Download a free exercise app on your phone and use it!
- Purchase a DVD you can work out to at home.
- Sleep – getting enough sleep is essential. Lack of sleep has been associated with weight gain and fatigue.
- Use a book or app to log your progress.

Do not over-exert yourself and use equipment properly. Be mindful of your surroundings and try never to go out running, jogging, walking or even bicycling alone. Purchase activity appropriate shoes and clothing, and stay hydrated.

Get a book to log your progress and activities. This way, you can celebrate the small achievements and see the progress toward your bigger goal.

Date: _____ **Write down 3 things** that went well.

Sunday

Monday

Tuesday

Wednesday

Thursday

Friday

Saturday

Why did these things go well?

Sunday

Monday

Tuesday

Wednesday

Thursday

Friday

Saturday

What Went Well?

Date: _____ **Write down 3 things** that went well.

Sunday

Monday

Tuesday

Wednesday

Thursday

Friday

Saturday

Why did these things go well?

Sunday

Monday

Tuesday

Wednesday

Thursday

Friday

Saturday

What Went Well?

Date: _____ **Write down 3 things** that went well.

- Sunday
- Monday
- Tuesday
- Wednesday
- Thursday
- Friday
- Saturday

Why did these things go well?

Sunday

Monday

Tuesday

Wednesday

Thursday

Friday

Saturday

What Went Well?

Date: _____ **Write down 3 things** that went well.

Sunday

Monday

Tuesday

Wednesday

Thursday

Friday

Saturday

Why did these things go well?

Sunday

Monday

Tuesday

Wednesday

Thursday

Friday

Saturday

What Went Well?

Date: _____ **Write down 3 things that went well.**

Sunday

Monday

Tuesday

Wednesday

Thursday

Friday

Saturday

Why did these things go well?

Sunday

Monday

Tuesday

Wednesday

Thursday

Friday

Saturday

What Went Well?

Experiencing the world **IS AN INSIDE JOB.**

Dr. Lisa Summerour

ACTIVITY #7
Mental Wellness

Like our body, our brain needs attention. We must be intentional about caring for our brains.

As you think about your day-to-day mental wellness, consider the following:

- Do something creative – coloring books, art or cooking class, reading, crossword puzzles, daydream, or anything that allows you to use your imagination.

- Dance! It increases the area of the brain that declines with age.[2]

- Create a space designed to help you clear your mind and relax. A favorite seat, with your favorite blanket, pillow and a great view, and daydream some more!

- Get outside and enjoy nature.

- Breathe. There are several breathing techniques associated with brain health.
    - Morning breathing
    - Renew your energy midday breathing
    - Relax end of day, 4-7-8 breathing

If you are struggling with anxiety, depression, anger, or have concerns that are adversely affecting your thinking or emotions, consider seeking a mental health specialist and get the support you need. You deserve to be healthy head to toe!

---

[2] *Frontiers Science News, Dancing can reverse the signs of aging in the brain*, August 29, 2017 in *Neuroscience*.

Date: _____ **Write down 3 things that went well.**

Sunday

Monday

Tuesday

Wednesday

Thursday

Friday

Saturday

Why did these things go well?

Sunday

Monday

Tuesday

Wednesday

Thursday

Friday

Saturday

What Went Well?

Date: _____ **Write down 3 things** that went well.

- Sunday
- Monday
- Tuesday
- Wednesday
- Thursday
- Friday
- Saturday

Why did these things go well?

Sunday

Monday

Tuesday

Wednesday

Thursday

Friday

Saturday

What Went Well?

Date: _____ **Write down 3 things** that went well.

Sunday

Monday

Tuesday

Wednesday

Thursday

Friday

Saturday

Why did these things go well?

Sunday

Monday

Tuesday

Wednesday

Thursday

Friday

Saturday

What Went Well?

Date: _____ **Write down 3 things** that went well.

Sunday

Monday

Tuesday

Wednesday

Thursday

Friday

Saturday

Why did these things go well?

Sunday

Monday

Tuesday

Wednesday

Thursday

Friday

Saturday

Date: _____ **Write down 3 things** that went well.

Sunday

Monday

Tuesday

Wednesday

Thursday

Friday

Saturday

Why did these things go well?

	Sunday
	Monday
	Tuesday
	Wednesday
	Thursday
	Friday
	Saturday

What Went Well?

DREAM ENORMOUS DREAMS.
believe they will blossom
AND BLESS
the world abundantly.

Dr. Lisa Summerour

ACTIVITY #8
Write Your Mission Statement

If you're thinking, I should have a mission statement? The answer is, why not? Organizations, corporations, and higher education institutions have mission statements, why not us?

A personal mission statement creates a filter by which you can view your decisions and your options. A personal mission statement can identify the gap between where you are and where you will be once you start living into your purpose. It provides clarity, creates intentionality, and direction that can help you get back on track when you get detoured. And more than likely, you will get detoured from time to time.

What to include: Who you are? What you do? How you do it? Who and how you serve or help? Why it's important? What are the outcomes? Review your answers from Activity #4 for information that can help shape your mission statement. Also, embrace the fact that without you and your gifts, the world loses something that could benefit others.

If you start your mission statement with "I am," you can also create an affirmation, which becomes even more powerful.

Here is my affirming mission statement:

I am uniquely designed to use my God-given gifts and talents to empower individuals by equipping them to embrace being fully engaged in their lives. – Dr. Lisa Summerour

Date: _____ **Write down 3 things that went well.**

Sunday

Monday

Tuesday

Wednesday

Thursday

Friday

Saturday

Why did these things go well?

Sunday

Monday

Tuesday

Wednesday

Thursday

Friday

Saturday

What Went Well?

Date: _____ **Write down 3 things** that went well.

Sunday

Monday

Tuesday

Wednesday

Thursday

Friday

Saturday

Why did these things go well?

Sunday

Monday

Tuesday

Wednesday

Thursday

Friday

Saturday

Date: _____ **Write down 3 things** that went well.

Sunday

Monday

Tuesday

Wednesday

Thursday

Friday

Saturday

Why did these things go well?

Sunday

Monday

Tuesday

Wednesday

Thursday

Friday

Saturday

What Went Well?

Date: _____ **Write down 3 things** that went well.

Sunday

Monday

Tuesday

Wednesday

Thursday

Friday

Saturday

Why did these things go well?

Sunday

Monday

Tuesday

Wednesday

Thursday

Friday

Saturday

Date: _____ **Write down 3 things** that went well.

Sunday

Monday

Tuesday

Wednesday

Thursday

Friday

Saturday

Why did these things go well?

Sunday

Monday

Tuesday

Wednesday

Thursday

Friday

Saturday

LEARN TO RECEIVE WITH *gratitude and grace.* RESET THE EQUILIBRIUM IN **THE WORLD AROUND YOU.** *others have been blessed* WITH GIFTS, TALENTS AND LOVE. **LET THEM SHARE THEM.**

• • •

Dr. Lisa Summerour

ACTIVITY #9
Give Thanks and Thank Yous

When is the last time you received a heartfelt and specific "thank you?" Do you remember how good it felt to hear someone say, "Thank you" or to read a thank you message? When was the last time you sent a thank you note, or said thank you to someone else?

For this activity, it's all about you giving thanks. It's about you giving "thank yous." To help you create your list of people to thank, imagine that you are receiving a lifetime achievement award. You are writing your speech, and you are listing all of the people in your life you want to thank. Who would these people be? Teachers, family members, friends, co-workers, employers, mentors, a religious leader, babysitter, or coach. You get the idea. Write a list.

Next, consider a few ways you can say thank you. You can send cards, an email, or flowers. You can make a telephone call or a visit. Get creative; what about a singing telegram, show tickets, a surprise lunch or dinner date? Make it as straightforward or as elaborate as you'd like.

Now, what to say? Be sincere, specific, and personal. Tell the person what they did to receive a thank you. Share how what they did affected you. You can even share why it was important that you say thank you.

OK, get your list, get some stamps and get started with your Thank Yous!

Date: _____   **Write down 3 things** that went well.

Sunday

Monday

Tuesday

Wednesday

Thursday

Friday

Saturday

Why did these things go well?

Date: _____ **Write down 3 things** that went well.

Sunday

Monday

Tuesday

Wednesday

Thursday

Friday

Saturday

Why did these things go well?

What Went Well?

Date: _____ **Write down 3 things** that went well.

Sunday

Monday

Tuesday

Wednesday

Thursday

Friday

Saturday

Why did these things go well?

Sunday

Monday

Tuesday

Wednesday

Thursday

Friday

Saturday

What Went Well?

Date: _____ **Write down 3 things that went well.**

Sunday

Monday

Tuesday

Wednesday

Thursday

Friday

Saturday

Why did these things go well?

Sunday

Monday

Tuesday

Wednesday

Thursday

Friday

Saturday

What Went Well?

Date: _____ **Write down 3 things** that went well.

Sunday

Monday

Tuesday

Wednesday

Thursday

Friday

Saturday

Why did these things go well?

Sunday

Monday

Tuesday

Wednesday

Thursday

Friday

Saturday

What Went Well?

Life is a journey. **HAVING SOMEONE WITH YOU TO EXPERIENCE THE** *adventures* **MEANS YOU CAN RELIVE THE MEMORIES TOGETHER FOREVER. THAT IS ONE OF LIFE'S GREATEST JOYS.**

— *Dr. Lisa Summerour* —

ACTIVITY #10
Purpose, Pleasure & Perspective

Have you ever thought about your purpose? Even if you never considered it until this very moment, there is something unique about you and how you show up in the world. I believe that because I believe this to be true:

> [4]Now there are varieties of gifts, but the same Spirit; [5] and there are varieties of service, but the same Lord; [6] and there are varieties of activities, but it is the same God who empowers them all in everyone – 1 Corinthians 12:4-6

PURPOSE: Consider what it is you have been blessed with in terms of gifts, service, and activities.

PLEASURE: Which of your gifts, service, and activities brings you joy when you are actively engaged?

PERSPECTIVE: What is the unique perspective you bring when you show up with your gift, service, or activity?

Hopefully, this will help you start thinking about how you see yourself in the world and realizing that the world needs you.

Date: _____ **Write down 3 things** that went well.

Sunday

Monday

Tuesday

Wednesday

Thursday

Friday

Saturday

Why did these things go well?

Sunday

Monday

Tuesday

Wednesday

Thursday

Friday

Saturday

What Went Well?

Date: _____ **Write down 3 things that went well.**

Sunday

Monday

Tuesday

Wednesday

Thursday

Friday

Saturday

Why did these things go well?

- Sunday
- Monday
- Tuesday
- Wednesday
- Thursday
- Friday
- Saturday

What Went Well?

Date: _____ **Write down 3 things that went well.**

Sunday

Monday

Tuesday

Wednesday

Thursday

Friday

Saturday

Why did these things go well?

Sunday

Monday

Tuesday

Wednesday

Thursday

Friday

Saturday

What Went Well?

Date: _____ **Write down 3 things** that went well.

Sunday

Monday

Tuesday

Wednesday

Thursday

Friday

Saturday

Why did these things go well?

Sunday

Monday

Tuesday

Wednesday

Thursday

Friday

Saturday

Date: _____ **Write down 3 things that went well.**

Sunday

Monday

Tuesday

Wednesday

Thursday

Friday

Saturday

Why did these things go well?

Sunday

Monday

Tuesday

Wednesday

Thursday

Friday

Saturday

What Went Well?

ACT ON IT OR *your* AFFIRMATIONS COULD BECOME *afterthoughts.*

Dr. Lisa Summerour

ACTIVITY #11
Be a Tourist in Your Town!

Congratulations! You are at the 11-month mark in your **What Went Well?** Journal. If you've missed a few days, it's ok. You've gotten this far and that's huge.

The "Be a Tourist in Your Town" activity is just that. Pretend you are visiting your town, city, area, and create an adventure that you think would be fun for a first-time visitor. You might plan to visit attractions, museums, a historical site, cultural centers, or take a tour or two. The goal is to select experiences you have either never done or experiences you haven't done in years.

You can decide if you want to make it a day or an entire weekend. Do you want to stay at home and venture out, or find a fabulous Bed & Breakfast, Airbnb, or cute little hotel to stay in during your time as a tourist? And, are you going alone, or inviting a friend or two?

Sometimes we miss the beauty in our everyday lives because we are merely moving through our days with a "business as usual" mentality. There are native New Yorkers who have never been to the top of the Empire State Building. Parisians who have never visited the Eiffel Tower. And Philadelphia natives who have never run up the steps at the Museum of Art and pretended to be Rocky Balboa!

Not you! You are going to venture out and have a local experience with the spirit of a tourist!

What are some ideas that come to mind of places you have wanted to see and things you have wanted to do? Write them below and start planning.

Date: _____ **Write down 3 things that went well.**

Sunday

Monday

Tuesday

Wednesday

Thursday

Friday

Saturday

Why did these things go well?

Sunday

Monday

Tuesday

Wednesday

Thursday

Friday

Saturday

Date: _____ **Write down 3 things that went well.**

Sunday

Monday

Tuesday

Wednesday

Thursday

Friday

Saturday

Why did these things go well?

Sunday

Monday

Tuesday

Wednesday

Thursday

Friday

Saturday

What Went Well?

Date: _____ **Write down 3 things that went well.**

Sunday

Monday

Tuesday

Wednesday

Thursday

Friday

Saturday

Why did these things go well?

Sunday

Monday

Tuesday

Wednesday

Thursday

Friday

Saturday

What Went Well?

Date: _____ **Write down 3 things** that went well.

Sunday

Monday

Tuesday

Wednesday

Thursday

Friday

Saturday

Why did these things go well?

Sunday

Monday

Tuesday

Wednesday

Thursday

Friday

Saturday

What Went Well?

Date: _____ **Write down 3 things that went well.**

Sunday

Monday

Tuesday

Wednesday

Thursday

Friday

Saturday

Why did these things go well?

Sunday

Monday

Tuesday

Wednesday

Thursday

Friday

Saturday

What Went Well?

IT'S OK TO PUT IT OUT THERE THAT YOUR LIFE IS WORKING FOR YOU!

•••

Dr. Lisa Summerour

ACTIVITY #12
12 Months of What Went Well!

Thank you for making the **What Went Well?** Journal a part of your life for the past 12 months. My desire was for this experience to be rewarding and empowering for you. My intention, through this journal, was for you to recognize that you are the cause and benefactor of beautiful things happening in the world. Know that the world needs you!

Use the questions on the following pages to help you think about and review the past 12 months. Please feel free to write anything else that comes up for you.

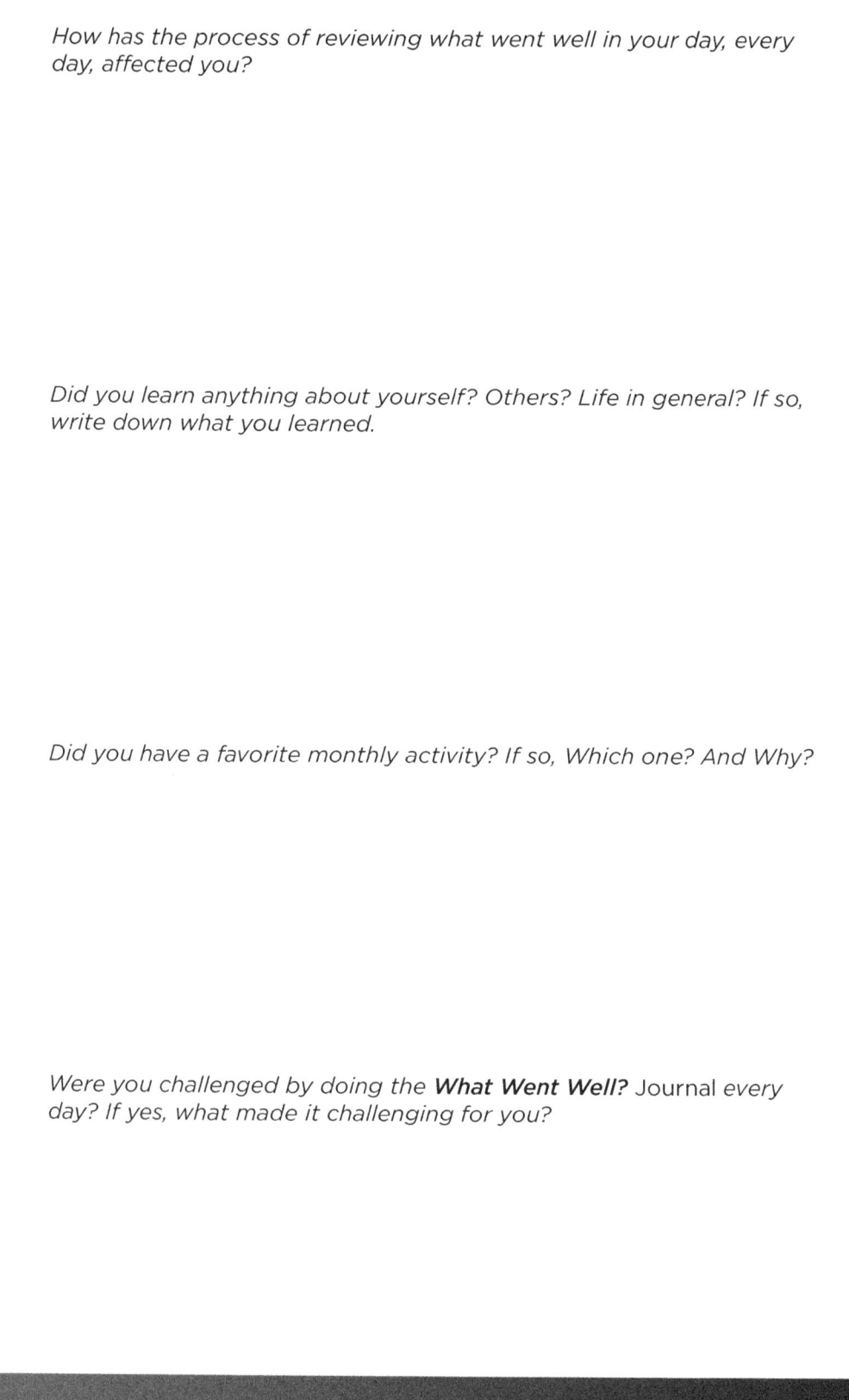

How has the process of reviewing what went well in your day, every day, affected you?

Did you learn anything about yourself? Others? Life in general? If so, write down what you learned.

Did you have a favorite monthly activity? If so, Which one? And Why?

Were you challenged by doing the **What Went Well?** *Journal every day? If yes, what made it challenging for you?*

Was there one activity you liked least? If so, which one and why?

What is a goal you can set for yourself that will challenge you and empower you?

Complete the **What Went Well?** Journal Survey online, to receive my FREE End of Year Review, which will help you assess the previous year and plan for an empowering next year.

Visit www.drlisasummerour.com/www_journal*

*Offers, information and access to assessments subject to change without notice.

NOTES:

NOTES:

I hope your **What Went Well?** Journal experience has been an empowering journey.

Connect with me for more empowering experiences at www.liveempoweredinstitute.com.

Connect with me on social media at:

Facebook: @DrLisaSummerour

Instagram: @DrLisaSummerour

Twitter: @DrLisaSummerour

Made in the USA
Las Vegas, NV
07 January 2021